CONTENTS

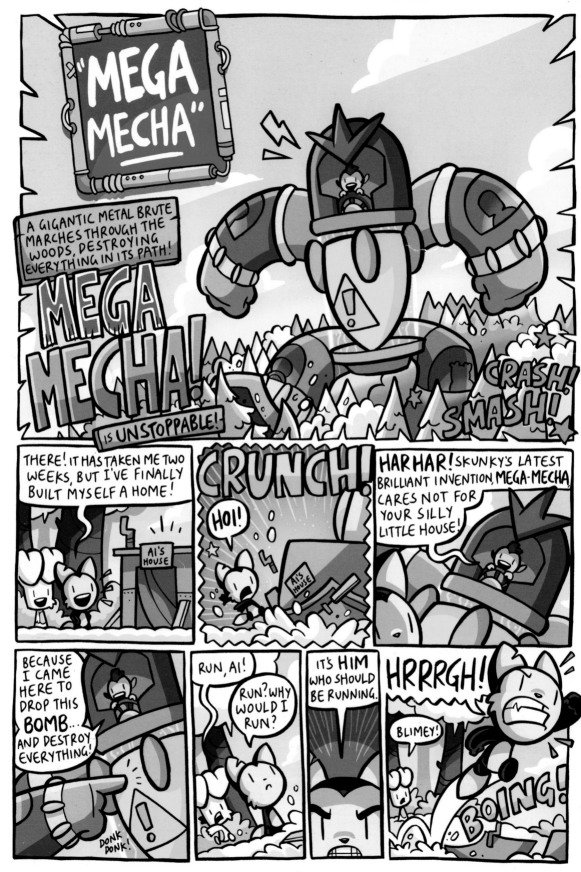

"TAKE to the SKIES"

WINGS?

CHECK!

BRRRMM BIT ON THE FRONT?

CHECK!

PACKED LUNCH?

CHECK!

SKUNKY THINKS HE'S SO CLEVER BUILDING THINGS, BUT WE HAVE MADE AN **AEROPLANE** ALL BY OURSELVES!

YAY US!

PIG, AS OUR TEST PILOT, HOW ARE YOU FEELING?

SHRUG!

HUH?

IT'S MY NEW THING! INSTEAD OF SHRUGGING, I SAY 'SHRUG'. IT TAKES A LOT LESS EFFORT!

SHRUG!

SHRUG!

SHRUG! SHRUG! SHRUG! SHRUG! SHRUG! SHRUG! SHRUG!

HOI! WHAT ARE YOU TWO UP TO?

WE BUILT A **PLANE!** YOU TWO? **HA!** BUT YOU'RE **IDIOTS!** AND I SHOULD KNOW!

WE **HAVE** BUILT A PLANE AND WE SPENT **WEEKS** DESIGNING IT AND WE'RE GOING TO FLY IT AROUND AND AROUND THE SKY!

February

A GREAT BIG SNOTTY "COLD"

AA-CHOO! STAY AWAY FROM ME, EVERYONE. I HAVE A COLD.

THPTHBTH! ME TOO!

ME THREE!

ME FOUR! CHOO!

YOU! FOUL SWINES! YOU'VE ALL GIVEN ME A COLD!

NOT SO FAST, MONKEY. EVEN **METAL STEVE** HAS CAUGHT A VIRUS!

BZZ-CHOO! BZZ!

IN FACT, THE ONLY ONE WHO STILL SEEMS HEALTHY...

PP-WINGGG!

...IS **ACTION BEAVER**!

CHOO!

WAIT HERE, EVERYONE! I'LL MAKE US ALL BETTER WITH **SCIENCE**!

DOWN IN SKUNKY'S LABORATORY...

WITH JUST ONE STRAND OF ACTION BEAVER'S FUR, I CAN ISOLATE THE PART OF HIS DNA THAT MAKES HIM IMMUNE TO THIS DASTARDLY COLD!

PLUNK!

I'LL JUST CAREFULLY PLACE THIS INTO THE **SCIENCE-A-TRON**...

FFRP!

AA-CHOO! EURGH!

AND NOW, WE PRESS THE **SCIENCE** BUTTON!

SCIENCE

BOOP!

"BUBBLE TROUBLE"

I HAVE DONE IT!

AFTER WEEKS OF EXPERIMENTING, I HAVE FINALLY CREATED MY GREATEST INVENTION!

... WHAT THE WORLD WILL COME TO CALL SKUNKY'S DOOMSDAY DEVICE!

WHAT IS IT? CAN I SEE?

ARGH! PIG! GERROFF!

BUMP!

MY DOOMSDAY DEVICE!

THP THBTH!

OOPS! BUTTERFINGERS!

WHAT ARE YOU EVEN DOING HERE? THIS IS MY SECRET LABORAT...

VMMMMM!

WHASSAT?

THIS PLACE IS FILTHY! ALL THESE BROKEN DOOMSDAY DEVICES LYING ON THE FLOOR.

VMMM MMM!

BUT... HOW DID EITHER OF YOU GET PAST MY SECURITY SYSTEM?

FLAPPY FLAP!

ABOVE GROUND...

SECRET LAIR

SECURITY

ZZZZZZZZZ

RIGHT! THAT'S IT! TIME I FINALLY DID SOMETHING ABOUT YOU TWO!

OOPS

PIG! DON'T RUN TOWARDS IT!

Hee Hee!

UH OH.

PIIIIIIIIIG!

CRUMP!

HE GOT SQUISHED!

HANG ON, WHERE'S HE GONE?

AH, THERE YOU ARE, HEINOUS SUPER VILLAINS!

PIG?

WHAT ARE YOU DOING UP HERE, YOU STUPID PIG?

ACTUALLY, MY 'STUPIDITY' HAS JUST BEEN AN ACT ALL THIS TIME.

I'M ACTUALLY SECRET AGENT P.I.G., INTERNATIONAL SPY, HIGHLY TRAINED AND WORKING DEEP UNDERCOVER.

WHAT?

WHAT?

WHUUUUT?

WITH MY GOVERNMENT-ISSUE HOVER TROTTERS AND LASER CARROT, I'M SUITED AND BOOTED TO FINALLY BRING YOU TWO DOWN!

BZZ-ZAP!

ARGH!

CLANG! ZAP! ARGH!
WOOSH!
CLANG!
STOMP!

NOW THIS MUST BE A DREAM.

OH C'MON, THIS MUST BE A...

STOMP STOMP!

PHEW! IT WAS A DREAM.

21

"A GIANT EGG"

HAS THERE ALWAYS BEEN A GIANT EGG HERE?

HMM, IT'S NOT ON THE MAP.

I'LL BET IT'S ONE OF SKUNKY'S EXPERIMENTS! ANOTHER DEVIOUS SCHEME TO HELP HIM DESTROY THE WORLD.

BEEP BOOP BEEP!

IN SKUNKY'S LAIR...

BRING! BRING!

YYY-ELLO?

WE FOUND YOUR GIANT EGG!

SORRY, WHO IS THIS?

IT'S, UH... BUNNY! WE FOUND YOUR EGG! WHAT'S IN IT?

OH, C'MON! I CAN'T BE EXPECTED TO REMEMBER EVERY HEINOUS EXPERIMENT I COME UP WITH.

EGG.

EGG EGG.

ARE YOU SURE IT'S MINE?

EVIL PLANS

WELL, IT'S NOT MINE.

WE'RE JUST LUCKY IT HASN'T CRACKED OPEN YET. IF IT IS SOMETHING I DESIGNED, WHAT'S INSIDE COULD BE ABSOLUTELY HORRIFIC!

CRAAACK!

UM.

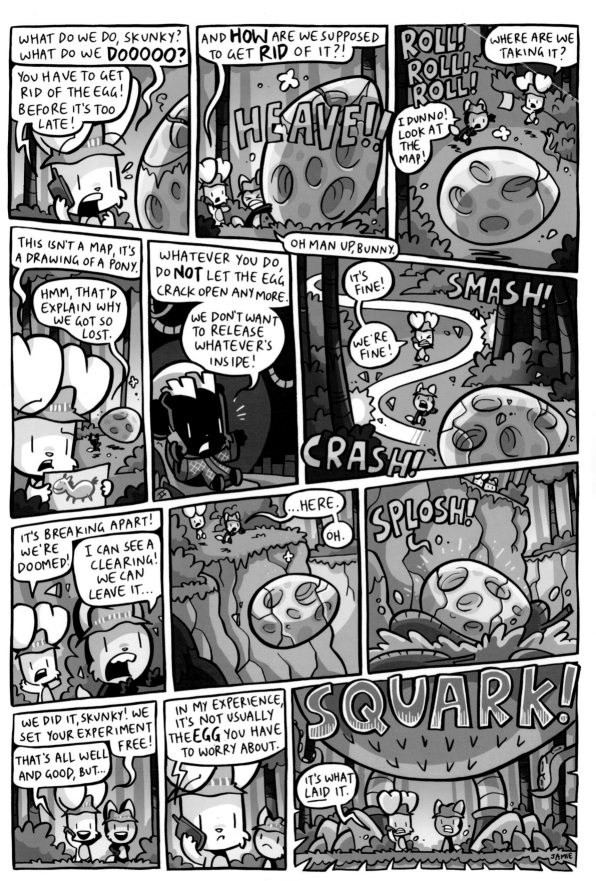

MARCH

"EAT UP"

SINCE YOU'VE ALL BEEN SO WELCOMING TO ME, I DECIDED TO PREPARE US A **LOVELY DINNER!**

YAY!

YUMMY!

OOP, HANG ON...

...DINNER'S ESCAPED!

ESCAPED? WHAT WAS IT?

WELL... **ANTS** OF COURSE! LOTS AND LOTS OF LOVELY **ANTS.**

ANTS?

BUT THEY'VE ALL RUN OFF!

CLANG!

UM... I DON'T LIKE ANTS.

HOW DO YOU KNOW?

WE AYE-AYES EAT ANTS ALL THE TIME!

IN THE FOREST I CAME FROM, WE'D TAP ON THE TREES TO MAKE THEM COME OUT...

TAP! TAP TAP! TAP!

HOI! YOU'RE BEING VERY ANNOYING!

CHOMP!

AAAAARGH!

24

25

SPAAACE

BYE! BYE!

GOODBYE, LOSERS!

IT HAS BEEN NICE ON YOUR PLANET, BUT NOW I'M GOING BACK INTO SPACE!

THANKS FOR COMING TO MY SEND-OFF!

IS THAT WHAT THIS IS?

HE PROMISED US **JELLY**.

BYEEE!

MONKEY, I HAVE DESIGNED THIS SPACECRAFT TO TRAVEL FASTER THAN THE SPEED OF LIGHT, TO TAKE YOU TO THE FARTHEST REACHES OF THE UNIVERSE.

PSCHHH!

YEAH YEAH, WHATEVER.

PSCHOO O!

IT'S VERY IMPORTANT YOU...

NEVERMIND.

AT LAST! FREE FROM THOSE DREADFUL IDIOTS!

WOOSH!

ONWARDS! TO CONQUER WHOLE NEW PLANETS!

FIVE MINUTES LATER...

I'M BORED. I SHOULD HAVE BROUGHT A MAGAZINE.

TWO MINUTES LATER...

ZZZZ

BACK ON EARTH...

COME IN, MONKEY. CAN YOU HEAR ME, MONKEY?

HELLO?

GROUND CONTROL

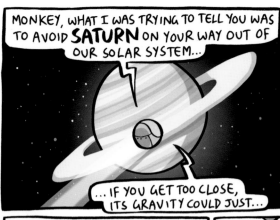

MONKEY, WHAT I WAS TRYING TO TELL YOU WAS TO AVOID **SATURN** ON YOUR WAY OUT OF OUR SOLAR SYSTEM...

...IF YOU GET TOO CLOSE, ITS GRAVITY COULD JUST...

...**SLINGSHOT** YOU RIGHT BACK AROUND!

WHIP-OOO!

AND **NONE** OF US WANT THAT.

SO IS MONKEY ACTUALLY GONE NOW? FOREVER?

I THINK SO. I THINK WE'RE ALL FINALLY **FREE!**

YAYYY!

ZNCK...HUH? **BANANAS!**

GASP! I MUST HAVE BEEN IN STASIS FOR YEARS!

WHAT AMAZING PLANETS WILL I DISCOVER THIS FAR OUT INTO SPACE?

BORNEO!

COR!

THE AMAZON!

FASCINATING!

GARDEN CENTRE, SOMERSET!

WHAT BIZARRE WILDLIFE!

EXIT

PLASTIC TREES (FAKE)

?

PLOOMF!

LANDED, AT LAST!

THIS PLANET SHALL BE MY NEW HOMEWORLD!

AND I SHALL CALL IT... **MONKEYOPIA!**

OH FOR GOODNESS SAKE.

ALL THAT TECHNOLOGY, JUST FOR TEN MINUTES OF PEACE.

"STORY TIME"

Once upon a time, there was a BUNNY in the woods...

WHAT'S THAT, BUNNY? CAN I HAVE IT?

GO AWAY, MONKEY! IT'S NOT FOR MONKEYS.

'BUNNY'S NOVEL'. YOU'RE WRITING A BOOK?

SIGH...YES, I WAS TRYING TO.

SNATCH

BUNNY'S NOVEL

WELL YOU'LL NEED SOMEONE TO DRAW THE PICTURES FOR IT!

HERE, HOW HARD CAN IT BE?

NOOOO!

SCRIBBLE! SCRIBBLE!

YOU'VE JUST DRAWN A PICTURE OF YOURSELF FARTING!

IT'LL BE A BESTSELLER! HYUK HYUK!

PTHBH!

Bunny hated Monkey. So, he tried to find some peace by hiding high up in a TREE...

BEES!!

AUGH!

28

AUGH! AUGH!

AUGH!! AUGH!

To take his mind off the multiple BEE-STINGS, Bunny decided to go for a walk...

SORRY, BUNNY!

OUT OF THE WAY! I MEAN, SORRY, BUNNY!

SPLUTCH!

GRRR! WHERE ARE THEY? THOSE TWO 'ACCIDENTALLY' SET ME INTO A JELLY!

MY POOR BOOK! I'LL NEVER FINISH IT AT THIS RATE.

CHOMP! RRRRRRRR!

SORRY, HE'S A BIT 'BITEY' TODAY!

NOOOO!

THIS IS MY BOOK! MY NOVEL ABOUT LIFE IN THE WOODS! AND YOU'VE ALL RUINED IT!

A NOVEL?

CAN WE READ IT?

And so, because all his friends were really stupid, Bunny gave up on writing and barricaded himself in his house instead.

OOOH!

I WONDER IF IT'S BASED ON ANYONE WE KNOW?

COME ON IN, WEENIE!

NOOO!

PIGS LIKE MUD, SQUIRRELS...

SPLUTCH!

...DON'T!

HA HA! LOOK AT YOU TWO, ALL MUDDY AND... ...MUDDY.

LIKE I SAID, YOU'RE MUDDY.

PIG? HAVE YOU GOT SHORTER SINCE YOU'VE BEEN IN THE MUD?

UH, I DON'T REMEMBER.

HEY, IS THIS SIGN RELEVANT TO YOU MUDDY NERDS AT ALL?

DANGER! SINKING MUD! STAY OUT!

AIIIEEE!

WE'RE SINKING, MONKEY! WE'RE SINKING!!

I'LL GO AND GET A CAMERA!

OR HELP! GET HELP INSTEAD!

OR BREAKFAST. I'LL GET SOME BREAKFAST!

GERROFF MY TAIL, YOU'RE PULLING ME...

YANK!

SPLUTCH!

...IN!

AHHH! THIS IS THE END! WE'LL ALL BE BURIED IN MUD!!

THPTHBTH!

THBTHPTHH!

DO YOU MIND? THIS IS SUPPOSED TO BE A SECRET UNDERGROUND LAIR...

OOH! BREAKFAST!

31

APRIL

"THE NIGHT THEY FLOATED OUR COWS AWAY"

HANG ON, GO BACK A BIT. **WHAT** WERE YOU DOING ON A FARM?

I... GO THERE SOMETIMES. TO HANG OUT WITH OTHER PIGS.

THERE ARE **OTHER** PIGS?

HUH.

BUT TONIGHT, **ALIENS CAME!** IN A **FLYING SAUCER!** AND THEY **FLOATED THE COWS AWAYYY!**

CALM DOWN, PIG. THERE'S NO SUCH THING AS ALIENS.

PROVE IT!

FINE. I WILL. BUT WE'LL NEED A PLAN.

ARE YOU **SURE** THIS IS THE RIGHT WAY, PIG?

I CAN'T SEE!

I'M A COW'S BOTTOM!

KEEP GOING!

32

ALRIGHT, LOSERS. WHO'S WINNING?

CLANG!

AI! YOU JOINED THE RACE!

YEAH! I JUST GREASED UP THIS HOLLOWED-OUT BOMB CASING!

I'LL PICK UP SPEED AS LONG AS WE'RE GOING DOWNHILL!

OH. WE STOPPED GOING DOWNHILL.

BUNNY

...TRAVELLING BETWEEN POINTS IN SPACE AND TIME AT INSTANTANEOUS SPEEDS!

WUB! WUB!

ARGH!

HELLO, BUNNY! WE COULDN'T FIND A 'VEHICLE', SO I'M JUST PUSHING PIG AROUND IN A BIN!

CRASH!

BUNNY 1

NOOOO! I'M SO CLOSE TO THE FINISH LINE!

IF I LOSE THE RACE, I'LL LOSE MY BET WITH MONKEY, AND...

FINISH

SWAMP!

HANG ON...

...WHERE IS MONKEY?

FINISH

SWAMP

HAR HAR! I TOLD YOU I'D WIN!!

VMMM VMMM

SPLUTCH.

WHAT? YOU WON? NO THAT'S NOT FAIR!!

FINISH

OH, AM I LYING DOWN ALREADY? THAT'S NICE.

BUT HERE, LET ME DRAW WHAT HAPPENS NEXT.

NO, MONKEY! GET OFF IT!

Then Stinky Monkey OVERLOADED the bogey gun...

click click click!

cool

...and it fired out the BIGGEST BOGEY in the ENTIRE UNIVERSE!!

Bloorp!

Hur!

THERE'S TOO MUCH ABOUT BOGEYS NOW. I WANT TO MAKE IT ABOUT ME BEING KING AGAIN.

NO NO, WAIT! THIS IS BRILLIANT!

Then Stinky Monkey ROLLED the giant bogey down the hill, before FLICKING it at BUNNY'S HOUSE!

Flickk!

"BLEURGHH!" Bunny said, like an idiot. Blugh! Eugh! GROSSSSS! Ha ha!

Bleurgh!

Ha ha!

But then SILLY PIG flew in and because he was in the SPACE POLICE he arrested Stinky Monkey!

argh! Nicked!

CLICK!

No he didn't! MONKEY RAN AWAY!!

But Silly Space Pig caught him!

thpthh!

Meanwhile, King Weenie was being great!

ALL IS WELL in my lovely woods!

argh! I fell in a hole!

duhh

THEN THERE WAS A DINOSAUR!

moo!

argh!

aiee!

eel

AND IT ATE EVERYONE!

MAN, I TOTALLY RULE AT COMICS.

JAMIE

CRASHING THROUGH THE WOODS AT A MILLION MILES AN HOUR, IT'S THE WORLD'S NEWEST FREE-RUNNING **SUPERSTAR**...

...THE UNSTOPPABLE **AI!!**

BO NK!

ARGH! ACTION BEAVER! WHAT ARE **YOU** DOING HERE? YOU GOT IN THE WAY OF MY LANDING!

BIBBLE!

TOO LATE!

I DON'T WANT TO HEAR IT!

I'M THE FASTEST CREATURE IN THESE WOODS, AND YOU WON'T HOLD ME BACK!

DASH!

YEAHH! NOW WE'RE COOKING AT **SUPERSPEED!**

NOTHING CAN CATCH M...

HONK!

HUH?

NO! GO AWAY! I'M **INCREDIBLY FAST**, THERE'S NO **WAY** YOU CAN KEEP UP WITH ME!

MAY

"DOUBLE TROUBLE"

GAHHH! I SHOULD NEVER HAVE LET PIG AND WEENIE HOUSE-SIT FOR ME!

THIS PLACE IS A MESS!

AT LEAST SOMEONE IN THESE WOODS LIKES TO KEEP THINGS TIDY.

ME.

HUFF!

DEEP UNDERGROUND...

EXCELLENT, SO BUNNY LIKES TO KEEP THINGS TIDY... I'LL NOTE THAT DOWN.

BUNNY

SURVEILLANCE SNAKE™, HEAD OVER TO AI NEXT.

SLITHER! SLITHER!

HIIII-YA! I MUST KEEP DOING MY MARTIAL ARTS TRAINING IF I AM TO KICK MONKEY'S BUTT!

DOOF!

HEHE, BUTT.

OKAY, MARTIAL ARTS, GOT IT. ONTO WEENIE AND PIG NOW.

AI

I CAN'T DO IT!

YOU **CAN** DO IT, YOU'RE JUST NOT TRYING!

THIS IS HOW THEY DANCE THE **SAMBA**! YOU JUST NEED TO PRASTICE THE STEPS.

HOP! HOP! HOP!

I DROPPED A PLUM!

DANCING... PLUMS. THAT'S IT, THAT'S ALL I NEED! THANK YOU, SURVEILLANCE SNAKE™!

NOW SELF-DESTRUCT!

SIGH!

BOOM!

AHHH!

WHY...**WHYYY** HAVE YOU BEEN SPYING ON THOSE IDIOTS? WERE YOU TRYING TO FIND OUT HOW **BORING** THEY WERE?

IT'S THE BORING, MUNDANE DETAILS WHICH MAKE US WHO WE ARE.

AND NOW, I CAN TYPE ALL THEIR INFORMATION INTO THIS COMPUTER.

BUTTT WHYYY?

TAP! TAP!

BECAUSE I NEED TO DOWNLOAD IT INTO MY NEWEST INVENTIONS...

CHUNK!

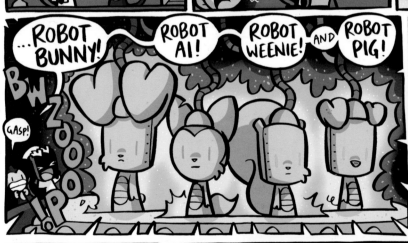

GASP!

BWZOOIPO

...ROBOT BUNNY!

ROBOT AI!

ROBOT WEENIE!

AND

ROBOT PIG!

WHO BETTER TO DO BATTLE WITH OUR FOES THAN **EXACT ROBOT REPLICAS** OF THEMSELVES!

GO, ROBOT REPLICAS! OUT INTO THE WORLD! WREAK HAVOC UPON YOUR ANIMAL COUNTERPARTS!

BZZ!

HIII-YAAA! BZZ!

SMASH!

TUT! LOOK AT THIS PLACE. IT NEEDS TIDYING!

BZZ! GO PIG!

BZZ! NOW THIS IS DANCING!

OKAY. MAYBE I MADE THEM A BIT **TOO** REALISTIC.

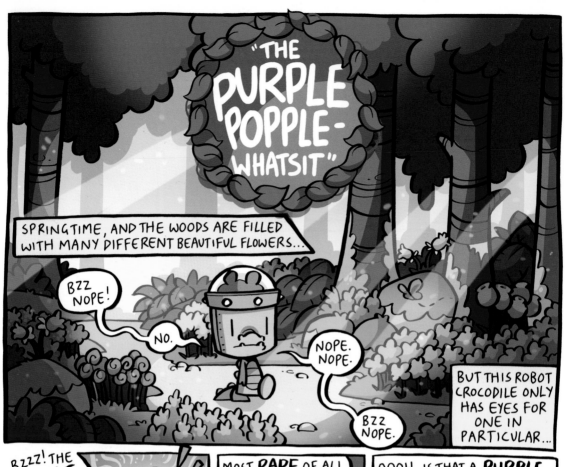

"THE PURPLE POPPLE-WHATSIT"

SPRINGTIME, AND THE WOODS ARE FILLED WITH MANY DIFFERENT BEAUTIFUL FLOWERS...

BZZ NOPE!

NO.

NOPE. NOPE.

BZZ NOPE.

BUT THIS ROBOT CROCODILE ONLY HAS EYES FOR ONE IN PARTICULAR...

BZZZ! THE PURPLE POPPLE-WHATSIT!

I'VE FOUND ONE!

MOST **RARE** OF ALL FLOWERS. MOST **EXQUISITE!**

BZZ.

I WILL PROTECT YOU.

OOOH, IS THAT A **PURPLE POPPLEWHATSIT?**

BZZ. HUH?

I'VE HEARD THAT THESE ARE RATHER DELICIOUS WHEN COOKED IN AUBERGINE STEW.

BZZT! NO!

NO ONE MUST TOUCH THE PURPLE POPPLEWHATSIT!

SCREAM!

BZZ ZAP!

IS **THAT** WHAT THAT FLOWER IS? PERHAPS I COULD SYNTHESISE IT INTO SOME SORT OF **PURPLE SERUM**...

...AND COVER THE WOODS IN A BRIGHT **PURPLE GOO!**

44

"SUN KINDA TROUBLE"

ANYONE ELSE GETTING TOO HOT?

NOPE.

IT'S WEIRD—WE'RE IN THE SHADE, BUT IT'S GETTING REALLY TOASTY.

IT'S NICE AND COOL UP IN THE TREES.

AIIIEE! MY SUN-LOUNGER IS CATCHING FIRE!

FWOOM!

AND MY FRIED EGGS GOT CRISPY BOTTOMS!

AWW.

UP IN THE TREES! THE TREES!

MELT!!

IT'S THE GROUND! THE GROUND ITSELF IS BURNING UP!

WHAT'S UNDERNEATH IT?

SKUNKY'S LABORATORY!

OF COURSE.

SKUNKY! WHAT'S GOING ON DOWN HERE? YOU'RE BURNING THROUGH THE GROUND!

EEK! UMM, I MEAN, NOTHING.

NOTHING IS HAPPENING.

SOMETHING SURE IS, AND I'LL BET IT'S BEHIND THIS DOOR!

NO! GET AWAY! IT'S NOT FOR YOU!

HEAT CHAMBER

CORRR.

WHAT... IS IT?

IT'S A SUN OF COURSE! I'VE BEEN PLAYING AROUND WITH NUCLEAR FUSION AND I ACCIDENTALLY MADE MY OWN SUN.

NOW I'M NOT SURE WHAT TO DO WITH IT.

IT'S A BIT HOT TO PUT IN THE BIN, Y'KNOW?

IT MUST BE BURNING AT A MILLION DEGREES!

29 MILLION, ACTUALLY.

WELL YOU HAVE TO GET RID OF IT SOMEHOW! IT'S ALREADY SETTING FIRE TO THE WOODS!

SNAP!

NOO! MY SUN!

CRASHH!!

BYE BYE, SUN!

SNIFF! REMEMBER YOUR DADDY!

A BIT LATER...

HOW LONG HAVE WE HAD TWO SUNS?

LITTLE WHILE.

HUH.

JAMIE

47

48

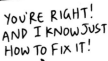

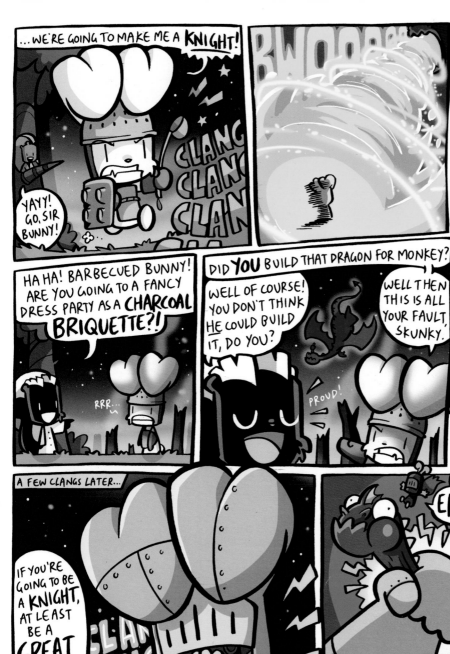

...WE'RE GOING TO MAKE ME A **KNIGHT!**

CLANG CLANG CLANG

YAYY! GO, SIR BUNNY!

BWOOO

ALRIGHT, WE NEED A PLAN B.

HA HA! BARBECUED BUNNY! ARE YOU GOING TO A FANCY DRESS PARTY AS A **CHARCOAL BRIQUETTE?!**

RRR...

DID **YOU** BUILD THAT DRAGON FOR MONKEY?

WELL OF COURSE! YOU DON'T THINK HE COULD BUILD IT, DO YOU?

WELL THEN THIS IS ALL YOUR FAULT, SKUNKY.

PROUD!

YOU'RE RIGHT! AND I KNOW JUST HOW TO FIX IT!

FIX... WAIT, WHAT?

A FEW CLANGS LATER...

IF YOU'RE GOING TO BE A **KNIGHT**, AT LEAST BE A **GREAT BIG METAL ONE!!**

CLANG CLANG CLANG CLANG CLANG CLANG

HAR HAR- ERK!!

GRAB!

BUT SKUNKY, WHY BUILD AN INVENTION DESIGNED TO DESTROY YOUR OTHER INVENTION?

I DUNNO. IT'S A LAUGH, INNIT?

SQUARK!

JUNE

"MONKEY LOOP"

SURPRISE, PIG!!

YOU THOUGHT WE'D FORGOTTEN YOUR BIRTHDAY.

FRRp!

...BUT ACTUALLY WE'VE BEEN PLANNING THIS SURPRISE PARTY!

NOT QUITE SURE HOW **MONKEY** FOUND OUT ABOUT IT, THOUGH.

YEAH! WHO INVITED HIM?

IF ONLY YOU KNEW.

IF ONLY...

YOU KNEW.

DRAG!

SLAM!

MONKEY! THERE YOU ARE! I HAVE JUST INVENTED A **BOUNCING JELLYFISH.** WOULD YOU CARE TO RAMPAGE IN IT?

NOPE. IT'S NOT SAFE.

WHAT DO YOU MEAN? IT'S MADE ENTIRELY OF RUBBER, IT CANNOT BE DESTROYED!

I'M TELLING YOU, IT'S NOT SAFE.

SQUEAKY SQUEAK!

FINE! **ACTION BEAVER?** TEST- PILOT THE JELLYFISH!

PLOP PLOP!

PLOP!

WOOP! WOOP! WOOP! WOOP!

P-DOINGG!

FFRP!

PWOOOOOOSH!

OH DEAR. DID HE JUST DISAPPEAR INTO SPACE?

I TOLD YOU.

BOOM!

MONKEY HOW COULD YOU POSSIBLY HAVE KNOWN THIS WOULD HAPPEN?

PARTLY, EXPERIENCE. BUT PARTLY BECAUSE—

I'VE BEEN LIVING THIS SAME DAY OVER AND OVER!

I FOUND YOUR NEW POCKET-SIZED TIME TRAVEL DEVICE AND DECIDED TO EAT IT!

DON'T ASK ME WHY, I'M A MONKEY.

IT DID SOMETHING TO ME. NOW I'M CURSED TO WAKE UP EVERY MORNING AND LIVE THROUGH THE EXACT SAME DAY.

I KNOW EVERYTHING THAT'S GOING TO HAPPEN.

FOR EXAMPLE, I KNOW PIG'S GOING TO BE CHASED BY BEES.

WORST BIRTHDAY EVER!

BZZZZ

I KNOW AI'S GOING TO HIT YOU WITH A BRANCH RIGHT ABOUUUT... NOW!

THAT'S FOR BEING AN EVIL SCIENTIST! NYAH!

TWACK!

BUT I DIDN'T INVENT A POCKET-SIZED TIME MACHINE! I THINK YOU SWALLOWED MY MOBILE PHONE!

BRING BRING!

¡BOOP!

HELLO, THIS IS SKUNKY FROM THE FUTURE. THERE'S NO SUCH THING AS TIME TRAVEL!

WELL I DIDN'T KNOW THAT WAS GOING TO HAPPEN.

NEXT MORNING...

I'M CURED!

JAMIE

51

"DOUGH NUTS"

SECRET LAIR (FIRE ESCAPE)

MISTER SKUNKY?

HELLO, MISTER SKUNKY?

WE THINK YOU WORK TOO HARD SO WE BAKED YOU SOME DOUGHNUTS.

HELLO?

HELLOOO?

QUIET, SIMPLETON! I HAVE JUST SYNTHESISED MY GREATEST CREATION YET!

PSCHH!

THE MULTIPLYER!!
JUST ONE DROP OF THIS LIQUID WILL MAKE EXACT COPIES OF ANY OBJECT IT TOUCHES!

SO...I'M GOING TO POUR IT ALL OVER MYSELF!

WHAT'S HE SAYING?

WHO KNOWS? I'LL JUST CHUCK THEM ALL DOWN TO HIM!

SHAKE! SHAKE!

★BOP!

TINK!

NOOOO!

(FLOPSY THE SENTIENT JELLY WAS RESHAPED AND NOW LIVES A VERY HAPPY LIFE AS A BOUNCY CASTLE)

"EVIL BUNNY"

TUESDAY, AND THE WOODLAND ANIMALS ARE BATTLING SKUNKY'S LATEST INVENTION...

BLAHH!

SPIDER CHOPS!

HRRG! YAHH!

IF I CAN JUST GET ITS MAIN CONTROL PANEL LOOSE, I MIGHT BE ABLE TO SHORT CIRCUIT IT...

MAIN CONTROL PANEL

AHA!

HERE I COME TO HELP, BUNNY! WITH MY WEAPON OF CHOICE...

...A SAUCEPAN!

HRRRR-EEEEK!

CLANG!

OH! I'M SO SORRY, I MISSED! ARE YOU OKAY, BUNNY?

BUNNY? I'M NOT...

I AM... EVIL BUNNY!

THE MEANEST TYRANT IN THESE WOODS!

AND I'M GOING TO RULE YOU ALL! BWA HA HAA!

I'M NOT SURE HE'S OKAY.

56

"THE BRAVEST SQUIRREL -IN THE- WOODS"

I WILL BE BRAVE.

I **WILL** BE BRAVE.

I WILL BE...

SHRIIIEK!

WELL, HOW DID YOU GET ON? ARE YOU BRAVE NOW?

IT'S -PUFF- NO USE. I CAN'T -PUFF- DO IT, I CAN'T BE -PUFF- BRAVE!

OOH, I'M GOING TO BE SICK.

NONSENSE! YOU HIRED ME, SKUNKY, MASTER OF THE MACABRE, TO **CURE** YOUR FEAR! TO HELP YOU FIND ~YOUR~ **INNER HERO!!**

AND THAT'S WHAT I INTEND TO D... GET OUT FROM BEHIND ME!

I CAN'T! I'M WETTING MYSELF!

HMM, PERHAPS SENDING YOU OUT INTO THE DARK WASN'T ENOUGH.

PERHAPS YOU NEED SOMETHING TO **REALLY** BE SCARED OF...

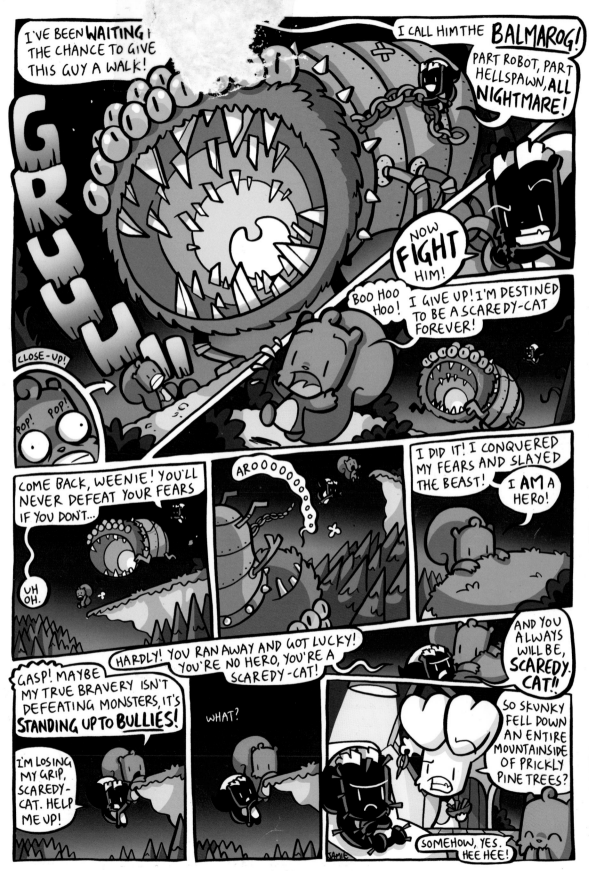

59